SCHOOL
of the
AMERICAS

SCHOOL

of the

AMERICAS

poems

DAVID RIGSBEE

Black Lawrence Press
New York

Black Lawrence Press

www.blacklawrence.com

Executive Editor: Diane Goettel

Cover art: "Rumor of Fire," © 2009 Jill Bullitt

Author photo: Jill Bullitt

Book design: Pam Golafshar

Published 2012 by Black Lawrence Books, an imprint of Dzanc Books

Printed in the United States

for Jill and Makaiya

CONTENTS

Acknowledgments

AGNI

Artful Dodge

Ce Low Press

Great River Review

Kaimana

The Brooklyn Rail

Café Solo

Poetry Hickory

Poetry Northwest

Pushcart Prize XXXVI

The Raleigh Review

1.

SHUM

I went with my teacher to a lecture once
in an ornate hall: long windows and Empire chairs.
The diminutive scholar was legendary:
he had been a confidante of Mayakovsky
and friend of the then-still-living Lilia Brik.
He had made formalism all the rage and so
blended nicely at Harvard when Stalin yanked
the choke-chain, and poets vanished in
binges of murder, imprisonment, and suicide.
We were late, and only a few unoccupied seats
were scattered about the hall. So down
the aisle we strode past more professors
than I had ever seen in one place.
Bearded, severe, they followed our entrance
with all the disapproval a Ph.D. can muster.
My teacher, a fierce blonde and former model,
countered with the aplomb of two well-received books
and parked herself on the front row, me next to her.
This distinguished professor announced that he
would recite a poem by Velimir Khlebnikov
by way of warming to his subject,
which was "sound verse," in Russian—shum.
Then he began to present what Khlebnikov
had claimed was a new poetry to counter

the tyranny of significance. Stepping gingerly
before the august audience, he started
to emit clicking sounds and to gesture
like an old-school Thespian. A silence went up
from the audience, unsure if it was
being played, or if it was just collectively
missing the boat altogether. At that point
my teacher reached into her purse
and extracted a compact and brush.
She opened the compact and gazed
at her own countenance for what seemed
a full minute, then began to brush
her hair with long strokes, pausing
every few to extract the captive hairs
and drop them on the university carpet.
The scholar pretended there was nothing
amiss and soldiered on with his rendering
of the poet's cricket impression, nonetheless
aware of the Amazonian woman not four
feet from him, so tall that in merely sitting
she easily matched his standing height.
When she had done, she put the brush away,
checked herself one last time, then snapped
the compact shut. With hands in lap
she sighed once and turned to the poetry reading
at last, letting her gray eyes come to rest

on the important little man and his recitation.
To this day, I don't know which was the better
performance. But each taught me something invaluable
about poetry, that art where I stood eager
to begin my work, that small country,
that Switzerland of decorum and peace
that lies between nonsense and vanity.

CANOE

Well into September the gardenias
were squeezing out their heavy smell
deep from the sugar of rot and pre-rot.
It was like Canoe, the cheap cologne
boys used to slap on their cheeks
before they went forth to meet the girls
who would pick over them (on this account)
and leave many in the emotional disarray
of having been passed over. But for some,
it was the smell of victory and reward,
and those grew sweet and strong, even
mythic, in the belief that nature,
or at any rate, their lives, possessed
a coherence that they could access
with their smooth skin, muscles,
and good teeth. No one suspected
any collusion with death, and only those
whom Giuseppi Belli called the "dog faces"
caught the faint decay that streamed after
the chosen swirled by, and even these
failed to draw any but a fair conclusion
because the moon was like that,
shining over the lawn, and the music,
although the words were inane,

pierced lovers and failures alike
with its silver needle moving in and out
of a fabric they don't make anymore.

IN PASSING

The artist I once compared to Ulysses
who learned to chisel frowns from quarried stone,
who painted ugliness like an angel
when the art world turned from the god-hunters,
high on infinity, in favor of the urban cool
of joke and technique, died an artist's death
on the throne, midday, disappearing from
the nurse's eye into the silence of marble.

Our last visit, he emerged, gloved and rubber-
aproned, pushing his jeweler's visor bought
to disarm glaucoma, up over still-thick hair,
pausing only to point the walker more narrowly
down the ramp to his sitting room.
From there, he commenced the last lesson:
space, contour, line, stepping forth into it.
He had lost none of the manic zeal with which

years earlier he cajoled Matta into buying
a used helicopter and brought from Italy
a Roman beauty, formerly a model, making her
dream self-creation so deep she slashed
canvas after canvas, until he showed her
how to find the ledge where space took off

and craft fell backward like a discarded barrel,
the space of the painting, I mean.

You're better than Schnabel! he thundered
at my wife, who, like a soul in Dante,
saw already the dead memory overlaid
on the old man sitting at her elbow.
She had come with her portfolio,
the student now grown powerful herself.
He urged her to study The Last Judgment
that ultimate in large-scale organization.

Look at Kline, he said, *though he doesn't
go far enough.* Always the plane: how
many dimensions to the plane? He hurried
to answer his own question. *Depth is not
optical,* he said, *and empty depth is not
space. When things are nebulous you have
to affirm the negative with clear images.
The deeper it goes the flatter it gets.*

The negative decides the contour. Hours
of this. Weeks later, I wonder how all
the cicadas draw down their racket,
then send it spinning back through the trees,
leaving dusk to sound, night to insight

because the negative space has to be positive.
And because it is evening back at the stone,
a small plane passing joins the mower.

NORTH STATE

My father came to me in a dream
to walk with me around a stadium.
Not wearing the jaunty motley of his last months:
the patchwork newsboy cap and paneled shirt
he wore when tearing around town,
   smoke streaming from the car window.
"I'm not gonna make it," he said.
"This may be the last time.
I don't have the breath for it."
We cried and smiled all at once.
The apparition faded, and I lapped the spot
before I knew. That morning
I had stopped to take some pictures
of a new structure: a five-story globe
affixed to a museum headquarters.
It was Sunday, the crews were gone,
but the wooden scaffolding clung
to the girders, "North State Steel"
spray-painted on each rib.
I had come before the planks were taken away
like cross-hatching erased,
before the world was made,
the panels bolted in place and painted
that planetary blue of earth from space,

that pendant marble
on which everything is always lost
like a glass eye that never sees
what it never ceases to watch.

THE STEGOSAURUS

His name was Butch, and I was his bitch,
that is, me, Mikey, Randy, Charles
and Kenny were, rounding out a handful
of chumps who came home through the woods
where he lay in wait and gestured us to understand
we were pussies until, the attitude escalating,
he punched us out with hickory-hard fists,
saliva flying from his hissing mouth.
He had fled the School for the Deaf
and hitched three hours to Durham
though he was unable to utter a single word,
signing and grunting until his intimidated rides
deposited him on his family's street,
which was our street. He never returned
to signing school, never learned a trade
but sat in a Barcalounger until he was forty,
and his parents had become ancient courtiers,
the only ones who intuited the wishes
of the lizard-lidded Nordic giant.
Company came and went, including myself,
and he would greet me by jerking
his head back a notch in a knowing way,
and let his eyes hold onto mine for a full second.
That was it: the peerless, punishing friend

of my youth lost in his boredom but sending
the ping of a message from the past
like a trapped collier who needed no skill
to show that silence and sounds compete
for the same stone, the one Yeats placed
in the middle of his great poem.
He pummeled the shit out of me one day,
while I was carrying my first library book,
a boy's story about a stegosaurus.
I managed to twist around and get him
in a headlock; nor would I release him
until his body conceded, and we lay panting
on either side of the path. That day
he acknowledged me by holding before me
his fist, which he then thrust into his pocket,
before departing. That day too I buried the novel
about the stegosaurus—I don't know why—
and made a note of forgetting anything
that happened to me until such time
as it made sense—me with words,
Butch with his massive arms menacing
the school path. It was late '62,
Kennedy and all just down the other road
and on their way into our new lives.

CHARLOTTE MEW

Something emerged from motes
the late afternoon sun had set spinning
inside a golden shaft. It was a lightning
bug too immature for the beacon
to have formed out the back of him.
Like a cursive "W" it made its way
looping across the space dividing
the nearer nothing from the farther.
I had been reading Charlotte Mew.
I was searching for a cadence of hers
that reemerged from the throat
of an older male poet some years back,
when I had sat in on his workshop
despite the obvious creeping dotage
just to hear stories and recitations.
Even at 86, he insisted on announcing,
in the alumni newsletter, every review,
every newly accepted poem, though
everyone already bowed to his eminence.
Not finding what I was looking for,
I thought it could have been
just my mistake. Such a loss
is not unlike a wind chime's
unrepeatable melody or someone's

aping a language they don't know.
You need the words, whatever else
bears witness to the dance in middle air.

THE HOOK

It was at the start of Neil Diamond's
"Sweet Caroline" when he sings,
"I can't begin to knowin'" that I first
realized the value of my education.
All those poems and novels were not
just there to be appreciated and added
to the store of vicarious emotions.
They were there to make someone
see what an ass could emerge from
the loins of self-creation, when
an otherwise intelligent man sought
to escape his hackneyed feelings
by torturing English grammar just before
the hook that would propel him
one summer into pop superstardom,
before the slide into camp
and weary self-parody. That summer
I was about to be married, when a girl
named, in fact, Caroline, began flirting
with me at work. She was nineteen,
a brunette, and I would come home
from work both exhilarated and confused,
for the first time feeling how the push-
pull of ambivalence might not resolve

itself in commitment predicated on loss
but be a destiny all by itself, a fate
of coming down squarely on both sides.
Reader, I married her—not sweet Caroline
but my fiancée. We saw Neil Diamond
perform the following spring attired
in reptilian leather, raised to a shine.
My new wife and I were far beyond
any real interest in such a sellout,
but for a Saturday afternoon outdoor concert,
it worked. A shower came up. Neil's skin
looked even more uncomfortable, but
showman that he was, he didn't betray
the mission. We covered ourselves
in a blanket, and the small cloud passed.
That night, I watched another show—
my body stippled in hideous hives—
the result of some allergen in the wool.
A few years later, graduated
and separated, I was driving in late summer
through western New York when I saw
Tesla's arcs, my first aurora, as startling
as hives. Sickles of light swept the sky
like a windshield wiper over the plains.
It must have lasted an hour. It had
come unannounced and unexpected, eerie,
but by then I knew exactly what it was.

FIELD SERVICE REPORT

Herbert wrote it was like "sweets
compacted"—about a day like this one.
May morning, little beings flitting
among weeds, songbirds refusing
to let traffic overwhelm their call-
and-response. I saw them coming:
Jehovah's Witnesses, two women
in long print dresses and two men
in black suits and black, wide-brimmed hats.
The women approached first, knocking
at the neighbor's door, the men
waiting on the sidewalk as if ready
to swoop in and shore up their efforts.
But there was no one at home.
I was sitting on the porch reading Cavafy
("Try to keep them, poet,/ those
erotic visions of yours"). In my mind
I had been transported to a little town
in upstate New York, where years ago
I lived rashly but deeply, full of
youthful longing, according to the time.
But seeing this formal quartet circle back
on my block, I closed the book
on Cavafy's vision and my own

and went inside. There I let the breakfast
dishes clatter and the radio music wail.
I didn't want to hear the doorbell
with its peremptory summons.
I couldn't bear to see the tired,
angelic faces at my door, arms
full of literature, such was my anger.

GIL'S SENTENCE

"Gil Scott-Heron to Be Sentenced"

—NY Times, July 9, 2006

"I find that rhetoric does my thinking for me,"
she said, turning the page, moving on,
having out-Plathed Plath, including
the bitchy conjurations of voice
that threatened to make all a trick
and fostered ill will. Next up, me.
I read my serious, inadequate verse,
remembering all the while the assassinating
queries of my undergraduate workshops:
"What is the function of the ego in this poem?"
"What does the third person mediate? Or is it
really you?" So often the poem came down
to you, and after my soft-voiced rendition,
silence followed suit, a reset button
before the class critic trained an interrogating
eye on one offending line. Elliott Coleman,
too aged and amiable to rein in
the revolutionary spirits of the seminar
pretended a real point of craft was at issue
and let the *sans-coulottes* have their way.

"It's sentimental," said one. "The subject
is unstable," said another. I had
no answer to these indictments and sat
silently, a you, while the rest of the eyes
wobbled back and forth as if not quite
believing their luck in having stumbled
on a massacre. Then a large black man rose,
I mean actually stood up and in doing so
tipped over his unlocked briefcase
spilling old cups, record albums, a copy
of his recent (published) novel and some spoons.
Scanning the table, he who had been silent
all semester debuted a serrated baritone
that wondered about the merit of intention,
something he thought neglected ("Intention is
the moon I follow," I seem to remember
his saying, though the verbatim trips here).
He was risen to that defense when justice
was poetic and of course snubbed me
later when I tried to ingratiate myself
with a little joke in our apartment elevator.
That other was about language: that was all.
But this was the weekend. He was in his
other world with his band, his other means.
Four or five menacing afros with shades
followed him silently up to a different view

of that white moon out in the alley,
beyond my place, beyond where I got off.

REDCAPS

In the poem a camp survivor
explained that while a certain poet
I happen to esteem believed
that at the end of the road
a Word existed to explain it all,
he, the survivor, offered instead the idea
that a silence, explaining nothing
was more worthy of a man of the world,
and implied the poet
was naïve to hold to his song.
I see it's a version
of what Kafka said: in the end
there's nothing ironic. No irony.
Think of it, reader! Therefore,
you're not permitted to write of that
region where the word stops,
but something lies still ahead,
be it God or death, or just the thing,
whatever it is, beyond the best thought.
You have only bread or tea or oranges
in a bowl, and even that drags
its privilege like an old steamer trunk
the redcaps rush to fuss over so that you
can look around, and regard the dappling

as more than shade, while they push
the weight onto the wagon.

ROY ORBISON, NEW ORLEANS, 1984

They were micro-operas, and he
was as lifeless a tenor, as could be
propped on a stage, so hidden in black
he seemed the emissary of oblivion,
except that there was nothing
he was capable of forgetting, no hurt.
He sang of disappointment straight up;
three blondes swayed to his catatonia.
I had separated from my wife
and appeared with my new interest,
a bi-polar space invader, as the years
would prove. On this lawn of denim
and tank-tops, we too moved
with the music. For Roy,
all of life's fullness survived only
in dreams, and because they did so
they were invariably sad, insubstantial—
yet within those boundaries, vivid.
Some years later I heard a fellow
read a paper at a conference.
His thesis was that Roy projected
a *posthumous* persona: the immobile,
obsidian figure drawing audiences
to that quavering falsetto, a voice

from beyond the grave, as warbly
as the gibbering, bloodthirsty ghosts
in Virgil. I mean, it was clever,
and I've thought of his point often.
Who doesn't wish, in some sense,
to talk back at experience
from the perspective of the concluded self?
It is a voice devoutly to be wished
that to the hearer would be a haunting;
to the singer, proof positive.
My ex-wife remarried, and to her
I am just a short that spun its way out
before the ponderous feature starring
a regular guy. My girlfriend got help,
but not before the worst
had befallen us, not before we said
what no earthly beings could take back.
At the next stage, the lead singer
had just taken his foot off
the wah-wah pedal like a driver
leaving the accelerator before applying
the brakes. Where did they think
they were going, the show-stoppers,
when the show was not in this life,
as we had just heard, and believed?

2.

GET IT DOWN

I had a friend who was so pathologically shy
he barely functioned in public. He was
in essence, a hermit living in a dune shack.
Unfortunately, he wrote poetry, and this
brought him to the attention of an art colony
that offered him safe haven, in return
for which he had only to push paper,
arrange chairs, and host weekly readings
by prominent poets. It was almost schtick
as he stood, a large man, before the gathering,
hands folded defensively over his crotch
and paused long enough to give
the audience, also, pause too before he swept
one hand mechanically, by way of introduction,
and blurted, "Miss Bishop!" or "Stanley Kunitz!"
then found his chair. It was a performance
of the highest order, in one sense,
and no one who was there ever forgot it.
He was a beautiful and mysterious poet too.
I said "unfortunately," only in the sense
that he had to overcome his shyness,
in order to look a fool in the eyes
of all. And I imagine him each time
going home from the weekly humiliation

to write the most radiant poems
as the green sea gnawed its way up
to the shack and the crabs scissored
across the wooden steps, as irrepressible
as I imagine Ritsos was, confessing
to his young executor, "You see, I'm
trying to get all this down before I die."

FLOW

It was an all-purpose body like Harvey Keitel's
that waited in the bar cave at the beach that year,
that girl upstairs, unsure of descending,
unsure of the purpose of purposeless leisure,
now that her children were grown,
now that they no longer depended on her,
except to bail them out of trouble,
as they kept slipping. Didn't they see
the budding mobster-cub in *Mean Streets* try
to guide his errant cousin away from the bullet
monogrammed with his name?
One way or another debts come due.
He wanted his cousin to understand.
Unsure and *unsure* were like
the levees between which the unstoppable
flow shoved its way to the sea.
That man was handsome, interesting:
he could talk. It might be he was
unlike the others. She remembered
that picnic she once went on, up on the levee.
She and her partner pulled over and parked,
then went for a hike along the tilting
cement. The river was predicted to breach
the lowest wall that night,

and looking out, it began to look
menacing and capable of things no one
had ever seen it do before. They sat
and stared at the river, then lay back
at a slant and watched the sky.
Before they even got close to the car
they could see something was wrong.
Someone had struck the window
making a black hole in the middle
of a radiant fracture, then reached in
to unlock the door. Naturally they
first rifled the glove compartment,
then pried open the trunk, helping themselves
to the picnic basket and booze. They even
took the ice chest that was full of mixes
for drinks they planned for the evening, later,
when they'd turned away from the river.

MINK

We passed on Mink DeVille and went down
to another club where studded, junkie coxcombs
leaned against old brick, profiled Mohawks
like halos in Fra Angelico, at maximum extension.
We bumped and snorted, then met the dawn
glazed with dew, under the bridge, immortal.

Last night, I lay awake listening
to summer's revelers hooting drunkenly,
occasionally rising to fist fights—until light
crawled across the ceiling. Then, following
a moratorium hour, came the sound
of street cleaners scrubbing stone.

I got it from my dying mother
how breath spaced itself further and further
between gasps until it was a new day.
A poet friend gave my old inamorata
six to seven years to live, max. I saw us
staggering around the Village, brain's ablaze,

swearing to hold our last meeting
in the same grave. Or so she said in a bar.
Those words, privileged, defiant, false,
also spaced themselves from previous words
until they fell silent—between us, I mean.
We met in a grave of words

but my fantasy kept a conversation
going about high and distant things.
That conversation gave shape to the eruption
of drunks howling on the pavement below
as they waited for the sweepers and the first
men in suits headed for the subway.

At the same time that spirit's rendition
was sweet nothings slobbered into a god's ear,
I moved at the heart of a deep reverie.
The times between being all ordinary saviors
needed to hail souls to 2.0, I couldn't help
noticing the smell of water on stone

and thought of Auden's face, the penitent
carved from the young man, the way a teardrop,
advancing from its source, destroys a mountain.

TALKING POINTS

Reading the autobiography of her
ex-husband, my now-distant friend choked
with sarcasm at the omission of herself
and the children, seeing that as conclusive
evidence of a man, not self-promoting,
but self-erased. During the dinner
at which he had proposed more than
seventy years ago, he kept a cheat sheet
of talking points underneath his napkin
in case the conversation lagged. Thus no
one was surprised when, at his death,
he had left nothing of his estate
to his forbearing survivors, but divided
the dragon's hoard between the library
and parks, and his late-life, buxom
caretaker spouse. It was pure Groucho
in the obviousness of it, but disbelief,
like belief, boils the frog slowly. At the end,
his sixty-year-old children still craved
love's table crumbs, but he who had made
of himself the exception was scarcely
inconvenienced by his own demise.
Surrounded by the attentions of children
still starving for a nod or a touch, he

waved them away to stare at the sea
where he experienced a warm, valedictory fog,
his body released in its brittle turn, showing,
how even at the brink, one could be both
immersed in the wretched longings of others
and blessedly devoid of empathy too.

THE MESSAGE

No one wants the explanation,
the letter droning on after the eye
has seized the message. Dr. Johnson
never finished a book, he said,
after he got the point. Why bother,
life being short and all? That's why I
once hung up on an old friend when
that fetid drop of sympathy began
to stain his discourse. There was no
point in feeling the muscle of the dead,
never again to rise and go forth,
never to walk by the river, or lie
on the grassy bank, the kind where
John Donne envisioned the soul in bloom.
When he called back, I hung up
a second time, hard. Johnson was right:
language is not enough. Literature
is not enough. When I first tucked
my girl in, bending over her curled form
with more than half my life, I heard
the storm of swallows cross overhead.
It was time, and they were at it.

RUSSIANS

It wasn't the end when
my girlfriend handed me the phone
in the middle of the night and said,
"Here. Say hello to my husband."
And it wasn't the end of anything
when another grabbed the wheel at 70
and screamed, "I could pull this
right off the road right now!
I could do it *right now!*"
Those frenzies have passed
into something like the memory
of a good novel, weighted in one's lap
when the day is cleared,
and there's nothing left to do
but look in on the Russians
passing out at the feet of their superiors,
emptying their wallets into the fireplace,
throwing their brain-stuffed heads
before the locomotive of History,
rather than face the vivid memory
of errors committed when the face
was hot and stared into the eyes
of that intransigent, that other face.

I AM NOBODY

Behind the blue house rises
two massive oaks still in baby green,
their trunks like petrified aortas.
Elsewhere the darker green of summer
takes hold. But for now what's most
at issue is drifting across
the still bright sky at sundown,
clouds showing their undersides
like mating animals. For what thing
does not desire appraisal? Even
the blue, famously indifferent
to characterization of any sort
makes a habit of being watched
by forest eyes, wary of night
more than the head who thought,
"I am nobody," as it leaned to the barrel
that day, a day that fell backward
like a vending machine off a cliff,
the whole damned thing styled for
impact, that from the rim above
seemed silent and tiny, barely a puff.

THE ASSASSINATION OF SADAT

I was probably the last in my group
to drop acid. I did this the day
Sadat and Begin shook hands and stood
grimly cheerful before assembled dignitaries
and press. Between that day and Sadat's murder,
I rode a black motorcycle to work,
my tiny, perfect wife perched on back,
reaching her model's hands around
my middle—a garland of her arms:
the bride I would lose with one
careless affirmative on a day
no calendar saw coming. Instant replays
were the thing then, and we saw it
over and over, how the assassins rose
from the reviewer's stand and took down
the President in a bloody, chaotic shower,
then sat down again, hiding the automatic weapons,
as Sadat and company walked backwards
over to the chairs un-overturning,
to the hero's greeting, then a moment's rest.
Before he was gunned down again
and the '80s proved the arrow of time
as willful as any bullet. The black bike
I rode I bought cheap off a guy

after an accident involving his knee
and hot, colliding steel. The insurance
made the bike, unlike the knee, good as new.
It was a time when I rode safe,
knowing nothing of anything worth a life,
knowing only that, after truing, the tires
followed the road on their own.
Which was, you might say, the last thing
I needed to know, a guy like me.

AT THE GRAVE OF JESSE HELMS

The siren travelling from one side of the city
to the other is like that trick
of stereo separation in the old
Moody Blues song about Timothy Leary.
Playing with your head: the bouncing
sound ball traversing the terrain
between your ears, cupped in phones.
He was probably right to hate us.
I saw the bullwhip handle jammed
in that guy's anus and knew,
in the larger sense, you could
lay the fault at my doorstep.
Of the nuclear family, Flaubert
conceded, you know they're right.
These days I see the campaign photo
of Mitt Romney, his wife and kids
smiling calmly at the voter. They know
which burdens styled whiteness eases.
They have no use for old tactics—
let the pornographers stamp them
with the imprimatur of kitsch. Let
the bullwhip protrude from the black
man's ass: there's no art in the fetish.
Once my dad took me to an orphanage

to shake hands with Aunt Bea
from *The Andy Griffith Show.*
Aunt Bea was indisposed; in her place
stood Senator Helms, greeting Shriners
with a snaggle-toothed smile and courtly way.
I reached up and took the hand that made
Gorbachev tremble. I tremble myself now,
and yet, who's to wonder at what
the imagination has to do—to say nothing
of the world we hoped to shape
with it. That was a long ago, but not
even death has moved the issues along.
The heart is still with Mapplethorpe,
the man superimposed on the boy and
pausing, before he steps into the leather shop.

MASHA

I'm listening to the violins shimmer,
a cheap and self-conscious attempt at
emotional presentiment, like Wordsworth's
daffodils—only black. It's perhaps only
a composer's joke (here, Rachmaninoff's)
so heavily does the music hove between
the quotation marks of what it feels, of what
in some way it must be, until it reaches
a chromatic delta, then regroups into
a swell of melody. To tell you the truth,
it reminded me—in the multivalent way
music does—of a time I drove to Montreal
to marry a Russian girl, Masha, so that,
like Auden's wife, she could peel off
immediately on crossing the border
and go her way into civilization, as Wystan
and Thomas Mann intended. I had been
put up to this escapade by a friend,
himself an émigré, and imagined its potential
far into the future, for literary treatment.
But what I found was a series of quizzical
beings, a mother, a sullen ex-husband,
and some other persons identifiable only
by grunts and movements in the background.

When Masha appeared, I beheld a woman
with a full mustache, a beauty
marred in an atrocious and pitiless way
not only by brutal politics, but
by something more hostile in nature,
something against which the mere
barbarities of the materialist State were
just buffetings of the otherwise inert.
We went for tea, and after listening to my
rehearsed entreaty, she told me in tenderness
and with tact, why this was a fool's errand,
why Canada, even with an ex-spouse in tow,
ended her pilgrimage more appropriately
than the States. I left as the sun eased
into the lake, feeling empty and ashamed
of using and also, of being used. I felt
like an aide-de-camp who had screwed up
at Yalta, having lost nuance and substance both,
and the second-to-last thing he remembered was
the swishing capes and the wheelchair's crunch,
as the principals exited the raised dais,
and everyone turned and glimpsed the Black Sea,
all swells and wheeling seagulls, one last time.

SODOMITES

So he's standing there on the porch
telling me how the Tea Party
is the true America, and I'm wondering
who's the bigger ass, him spouting
or me listening, when my stare
falls on his two brats running
in and out of the screen door,
two boys who will likely
grow up to extend the reach
of their dad's simple mind.
But then I wonder what
would happen if his side won.
How bad could it be not to be
on the side of the bigger truths,
not even on the side of facts, which
would seem some kind of default
but is not, apparently? It would be
to believe the truth is bound as a child
is tied to its mother while the stars
spin crazily in their silent voids,
invulnerable, waiting to die, as we
are, but unlike us, unencumbered
with the memory of their rise
and fall. Now he's railing against

the gay agenda and refuses to use
any term but "sodomite," which gives him,
he thinks, a kind of patristic armor.
But after all, he is family,
and I let him go on, without further
correction, as the kids breach the door
once more, and I can see
how they could kill me, a grownup
who bandies language. Theirs
are the small eyes that peered
from the dark of caves that belonged,
as they feared, to merciless animals
we know now only from renderings,
and then only sideways, never head-on,
as if the observers devoutly wished,
after recording them, they would pass.

ELSEWHERE

I'm listening to the same birdsong over
and over. It's what the bird is putting
out there from inside the scalloped leaf
layers, then borne on the hot air
of a quiet afternoon. Something picks it up,
in some other tree, not the same song, but
consistent with its hammering repetition, only
elsewhere. That's the thing, isn't it?
Elsewhere. When Blake explained that Christ
was Imagination, what else did he
have in mind, but that the Son of Man
was elsewhere, working on a new gesture,
perhaps a sign as yet unknown to commentators,
which looked at first like legerdemain,
slipping through a hole only he could see,
to turn around in the air there, the highway
of birds, bearing witness, like any savior,
to its endless loops and curves.

THE ATTIC

I'd thought the steps had shortened,
but the stair looked as if the indifferent sky
itself had offered a rippling rope ladder
like one of those dangling uncertainly over
the side of a tanker ship, so steep
was the ascent, so unlikely the salvation
from the sea. But that was a trick
of perception. True, the folding ladder
was shy a rung, its legs so far from straight
I imagined the odd, reversed knees of beasts,
before focusing on the rectangular hole,
like a inverted grave, upward into darkness.
Once there, I made my way over boxes,
the annals and souvenirs: pictures pocketed
in bill-flapped envelopes—dozens—yellow
on black like barriers at construction sites.
Then correspondence, some bundled and tied,
as if themselves in families, some loose, shiftless;
then envelopes alone, just a step above
empty wrappers; then more letters shed
of their envelopes, still making entreaties.
Past row on row of such a congeries, such remains,
I crawled like Nebuchadnezzar in that Blake
engraving, naked, self-absorbed, alone with rodents

that scratched and tumbled behind barriers,
along ledges and beams. It was there I found—
furnace ducts crisscrossing in secret order
like a train yard—the metal box that held
the means that took you. It called to me
like a heart carried over continents and centuries—
Shelley's or some totem encased by saints
in Boccaccio. But this terrible heart was forged.
I knew it was there, how it had followed me
year by year, from house to house.
I remembered just where among the junk.
On hands and knees, I approached, supplicant,
knowing how long it had waited, box worthy
of some hero, not me, but I couldn't help myself.
As if waiting for the moment to widen and
let me in, I reached out my hand in love.

3.

ODE TO WILBUR MILLS

"He can't speak with you now, he's on the floor."

When the house next door went up
for sale, I wondered about the children
racing through the garden maze,
two little boys and a tiny girl
skimming the boxwoods. Now another
yard sign appears across the street
before the lawyers' house with its blue gingerbread,
"New Price" affixed like a Post-It
(I didn't know there was an old one).
A workman's wooden ladder directs
the eye to messed, rotted shingles
and mottled underlayment
above the porch and a man there,
hands on hips, surveying the job ahead.
What if my poems find no place?
What if the house changes hands
and the ladder comes down
when all is fixed and rearranged,
when the oak behind the blue house
towers and becomes, for a moment, still?
I stare at sameness and seem to see
back through the layers, and the thought

comes to me of Wilbur Mills
giving a press conference from the dressing room
of his stripper darling,
the ruinous audacity that drew
a blessing—the silent applause of divinity.
I remember his bespectacled face
emerging from its mask after thirty years
to squint from the past into the camera,
and the idea likewise emerges that
it's like that, the peering beyond thinking
of the god of love, the terrible god
of faith and wreckage.

TREEHOUSE

I look up and imagine living in the tree,
not as a squirrel starting, fidgeting
before a mortal leap, or as a crow
keen to fold its negative parasol,
still less an owl in whose stereopticon
no grace intrudes to rescue prey.
But I would climb up, as I did
with my brother, and build a treehouse
in the sweetgum limbs. The twisting
slats in our ladder led to the level
planks from which rose walls and ceiling.
There was even a window, put in
with much effort, to keep an eye
on trouble which, like innocence,
was always by and loved the shade
we cast, a reverse spotlight into which
it stepped like the host of an old variety
show to have us know it was starting.

AFTER ALL

I once had a girl, sang the Beatles.
I had one who was high maintenance,
though she admired a local man
who ripped engines from new Jaguars
and replaced them with Chevy V-8s—
so unlike her own philosophy.
I loved her for the troubles, although
of course they became a liability by and by.
Even as my poem takes shape,
drying on the legal pad, I note
that some expressions ("although"
"of course," "by and by") exist only
to true the bias of neighboring words.
Before you know it, a tale is spun,
a form imposed, and feelings
imprisoned. Dostoyevsky
could not have come up
with a more disturbing heroine
than the one who emerged
from our falling in together.
It would be merely literary
to provide examples here of her
vitriol: many was the time I stiffened at it,
only to be melted by an artless word.

If it is possible to forgive
such a woman and in the process
to forgive myself why do I
hang back? I thought she was
peerless, the real deal. What was
I thinking, you may rightly ask?
When you stop to consider it,
everything is a test. In failure
you step forth just like the beloved
in the Shakespeare sonnet, except
that you aren't the beloved anymore.
You are just a person who has incurred
certain consequences that fold in
with natural changes and after a while
become indistinguishable from them.
If it is possible to forgive,
doesn't the pain return for another bow?
Doesn't the feeling of degradation likewise
follow the memory of drama?
I had learned from Mozart
that forgiveness is an attribute of deity:
Lazarus coming back from decomposition
at the summons of Christ;
Semele unblasted, her limbs refitted,
the gorgeous head reattached to its neck
before the presto of reanimation

and the trudge to Olympus. And yet,
isn't it said that the torn sing anyway,
the head as in a trance, slowly mouthing
the O of astonishment at having
returned to life, for what
could that life hold in this
new limbo? It was, after all,
just an idea of the more aggrieved.
After years, my girlfriend did get help
and yet, as Lowell remarked,
how terrible that such *Sturm und Drang*
resulted from a salt deficiency. I forgave
with what limited motive I could muster,
but she did not return to my life.
She was happy with the life she had
working on her golf swing
with her CEO husband. And I
was left to contemplate my partial act,
that bomb against nature
that didn't go off because only the trigger
ignited. But nature doesn't want
the return of the dead. Only we
do because the heart is an ironist,
which is to say, a nihilist,
because it will go to its grave believing
we were nibbled by happiness,
when sadness swallowed us whole.

MAGIC MARKER

In my memory I hear the voices of poets
I knew or read years ago, fearing
the coming muteness of their verses,
their growing irrelevance in snow after snow,
storm after storm and even more, the long,
monotony of unassisted time, the triumph
of inertia over will. Japanese
maples filter the sunlight into infinite
gradations until, as noon passes over
into afternoon, that green shade
in the Marvell poem unites with
the green thought somewhere in imagination's
forest. It's here those voices rise
into a soughing that almost immediately
subsides. When she knew death was
soon to come, a former artist's muse
told me that whenever she saw
a sign that proclaimed, *Jesus Saves,*
she would pull over and reach
for a Magic Marker she kept in the console
for just such occasions, and making
her way to the sign in question
would add the single word: *string.*

SCHOOL OF THE AMERICAS

I forgave my aunt for boasting she knew
Lt. Calley and for banishing her daughter
to a home for unwed mothers at nineteen
(finishing school was the phrase we heard).
The girl, now nearing middle age, would be
somewhere in America. But where?
New facts show their traction now
that these relatives have died off
and left the home stretch unimpeded
by their last emergencies. What I couldn't
forgive was the time this aunt woke
my brother and gripping him by the forelock
hissed he was "stupid" to have kicked
my uncle, a full colonel, the day before,
as he made ready to leave for his job
with the infamous School of the Americas,
where he taught history to killers.
He met the blow with a look and made
no reply, but reinstated the military tone
with such enhanced indifference
we came to regret our vacation there.
That summer I pursued my cousin,
an in-the-know pre-teen who had already
trained a brown doe-eye on boys.

My brother moped and never after
seemed as triggered by mischief.
My uncle took his pension by an Arnold
Palmer course near the base,
a retired general on the far side
of the water trap. I couldn't forgive
whatever it was that planted the cruelty
in her voice—or my uncle's silence.
But the butterfly effect, secret timing,
and indirection spread and toughened
death's vine. If to forgive is to
bring back to life, let them lie
in the peace of mistaken privilege,
if peace it is. As for me, I can't
and I don't. Let death be the lesson
again, as it was in the beginning,
so that what it is without them
unfolds in love's stead, under the sky
where I lie back, eyes open, taking
into my body breath that is all mine.

SONG FOR TOM

Let's say Jesus made an offer:
the songs but without the voice—unless
you count a finishing sandpaper
voice drier than Dylan's, less able
to hold a note than Leonard Cohen's.
Would anybody give his whole life,
complete with anonymity, disease,
divorce, penury—to accept such a gift?
"Some nights I can't feel my feet," you said,
"when I'm performing." Here you swept
your freckled arm as if to say, "All this..."
revealing street shoes flat-footed
next to a barstool. "I'm afraid I'll topple
from the stage and crash on a drunk
divorcée at the first table." When Esquire
profiled you in the '90s I thought
at last for your sudden fame erupting
from the obscurity we shared.
Eventually, obscurity lapped the fame,
but the fame flexed into myth
and when I saw you last, now forty years on
in uncharitable Nashville, you
had just sold the rights to your catalog
in return for future deals, nominal,

niche, your record company a website.
You still trekked by bus to Calgary
or some South Carolina hamlet
just to let a college or a local jock
have at you for an evening. By the time
you had bought it all with flesh's coin
you were a coterie star. And when
the musicians sat around, you observed,
there was no way to stanch the booze.
Jarrell remarked how in driving out
our demons we should beware
of driving off our angels too.
It is the obligation of service,
you explained, to propitiate the angels.
So like the shards they sing of,
your songs reclaim the territory,
the torn maps, creased trailers,
the sadism of the banal against which
real yearnings cross, forging destinies
from lives as memorable as wallpaper
in songs as sturdy as Biblical wood.
Such your genius, to rasp our fiascos
far out into that other world
that, like the part in Jimmy Carter's hair,
reverses the whole head, and all that stands
behind that head—a fact detected

when a photographer from the press pool
compared the newest negatives
with all the stock on file.

BALD MAN WITH POODLES

When the cemetery trees were pinched
over by the storm that day, their rootballs
rose and sat like strange, hairy globes
of dirt and rotted wood, and beside them,
the freshly excavated craters where once
they stood. The first to arrive were afraid
to look in, for fear some protruding bone
would confirm how wanton was air
in the service of death, and so snatch
the boutonniere from the lapel of the man
walking by, the bald man with a poodle
attached to each arm. Everyone knew
his mate abandoned him; no one knows
why. In spite of the trees he walks by.
It is the ordinary that sucker-punches.
Sunlight ricochets off his shiny head.
The dogs, like animals made from balloons
by an unfunny clown at a children's party,
would prefer the smell of turds and grass
to affection given on account of their beauty.

HERESIES OF SELF-LOVE

I have known more narcissists
than is healthy for a man my age.
They've come in all sizes and shapes
but they've had one thing in common:
they lacked the ability to imagine
briefly that they were not themselves,
which in just about any shorthand
translates to a lack of imagination.
And yet, it was seldom unadulterated,
that love; rather it was a desire to self-
dance, as Shahid used to do in clubs,
a student assistant designated
to chauffeur and then to follow him
onto the dance floor with—I kid you
not—a full-length mirror so that
he could enjoy himself to the max.
Or take my friend, the visiting writer
in but one of a thousand skirmishes,
scoring points off a prissy senior
professor who rose to take issue
with her at dinner. "George," she
said, slicing the table with the blade
of a look, "you say *one-grotesque-thing-
after-another.*" As a poet friend said,

when I told him this story—how she had
dissed modesty with a flick: "She is
a very stupid woman." They were performers,
and we felt delighted at what seemed
an unreachable freedom. But not all
were so entertaining as to be merely
benign. Blake, who is infallible in such
matters, said that Satan is the ego,
the imagination's surrender to bounds.
My college roommate bears this out:
an only child, he learned self-love so
hopeless and pure he wouldn't kiss girls
unless they brushed their teeth first,
for which purpose he brought along,
and handed over, a spare toothbrush,
then waited on the makeout couch
for their return, if they bothered.
If they didn't, no matter. When I
happened to mention an attractive
classmate who had given up art
to marry a much older Florida man,
he replied without a hint of irony:
"I copulated with her once."
Nor did other than natural fabric
touch his epidermis. Even boiled cotton
seemed an insult, as I learned once

on a boat ride at Kerr Lake when he
stripped off the lavalava covering
his vitals before my startled wife,
then posed, an escaped art-class model
buck-naked on the prow of the motorboat,
hands on hips, eyes on the horizon,
as tethered skiers skipped by.
I was sure we'd all regret our ill-
starred vacation when the Coast Guard
turned us over to the vice squad.
But even a temple falls into disrepair
when the last priest enacts the aging
of window and beam. Like my superior
colleagues, I used to frown at these
lurid cautionary tales, but nowadays
what I really regret is the way
the parallel lives erased my own.
I smiled at the bravado and the times
remembered because of an image or a story.
But when I speak to this past
and hope to hear my name returned
in the voice of another, what I get
instead is the sound of tires slicing wet
pavement, and maybe there's a wind
lifting the heavy racks of leaves
and letting them down again,

maybe a bird hunched and invisible
near the dry trunk, the shielding
bark, whose song is the bread-
and-butter of any strange, nighttime fowl.

THE SLUG

When they found him in bed,
facing up, the police were hesitant
to rule my brother's death a suicide.
The pistol lay there yes, in his left hand
and yes, there was an exit wound
so blood had equal opportunity to sop
the bed from either side and mix its
metallic odor with the smell of gunpowder.
But any habitué of CSI would know
the perp will remove the bullet, if possible,
and so the cops were suspicious,
unwilling to say what we feared most.
Instead, they bracketed their skepticism
and went about collecting other evidence,
taking samples and pictures, measuring
the ricochet crater in the dresser trim,
as his body lay, like *savasana* in yoga,
a difficult pose because you have to
commit to stillness against every itch
or urge to rearrange the limbs and bring
them into closer alignment with the inanimate.
They found the note, beer cans, rifled
files. I myself discovered the note too,
reversed, embossed on a blotter—and clear

only on the reverse side, so that you
had to hold the eerie dispatch to a mirror
and read it like Leonardo's journals,
those discourses disallowed to commoners.
But what could be more common
than the wish to spare more pain,
as halting words, especially, arrive
one at a time, to serve? It was not
until hours after the fact that
the coroner ordered the body moved.
Then they found it, the bullet. In its
journey out the .38 barrel and through
my brother's wits, it had bounced
like a pinball around the machine
of the bedroom, furniture its bumpers,
and come to rest. Falling back on it,
he had both hit a bullseye and written
a mystery before the lead was cool.
The cops were amazed at the dead man's
surprise and crowded around the slug
like miners around the Hope Diamond,
for whom, as with the real miners, there
was no profit to be had from finding
such a conspicuous, untradeable treasure.

THE COURAGE OF UNSPEAKABLE ACTS

My father spoke of it, hunched
there on the balcony. I offered him
a cigarette, but he waved me away.
He had officially kicked the habit
but he wasn't so good at hiding
his stash—at least not to me.
I had smoked a dead man's pack
that I found in a jacket: I knew
the day would come, and it did.
Not far away, a Confederate cemetery
got up in emblems and flags was but one
lost cause. The sons of my mother
were another, and one day my wife
turned to me at dinner and declared
my habits were a "slow suicide."
The phrase reminded me of the caption
in Bishop's poem about her timid aunt,
She remembered the phrase describing
a man slung on a cannibal spit: "long pig"—
what at *National Geographic* passed as wit.
The crack in the sidewalk soon finds earth.
There were sidewalks below us, but no
people. The smoke from my Lark merged
with the larger breeze. It was evening.

I didn't know what light my father
was looking at when he said,
"I can't get over the courage it took.
No one ever talks about it."
At that moment we were called
back inside, and I flicked the cigarette
into the night, kept the smoke in my lungs
as long as possible, like life itself,
then held the door for my father.

THE TRANSLATOR

He didn't have his own poetry
but he had that of others
which he translated. And those
versions became his *oeuvre*,
the work of his life, although
it was also the work of others.
In this way, he kept himself to himself,
and that public-private divide
others find both necessary and a great
human enigma (think Chekhov, Woolf),
he dismissed altogether.
His translations became famous for
their clarity and prudent word choice.
He won praise for not imposing himself
on his authors, but for disappearing
into the service of the art. What
nobody saw was what a great poet
he had become. His private life
was always the theme, and every
work was a masterful elegy for what—
now singing in an alien tongue—
it was no longer. In the end, he did
all that a man can do who wishes,
as Emerson said of every man,

to justify himself, who would otherwise
stumble on the way to success
and fade, unexpressed and obscure.

YES WAY

The studio was coming along. She'd had
racks installed to store the paintings,
an a.c. brought in to supplement the meager
cool that never seemed enough, when the sun
bore down and heated the blinds to scorching.
She'd rearranged the track lighting,
set up a stereo so she could listen
to chamber music there, in that chamber.
And an unbreakable lock: not to forget that.
On the other hand, there was the time
away, putting out feelers in the big city.
There were the close friends and death:
one gone and one waiting . No way
was there work to be done in the interstices
of these events. Then the hoary father
whose self-love was so indomitable
he threatened to outlast the room, as if
he might become, finally, the first immortal.
Why feel mugged by his demise?
She started to work again, to bury
him over and over, to catch
multiple caskets escaping in a black sky,
or was it to wave them on?
In any case, the sky cleared and there

was nothing in the way at last but
the self imprisoned in its freedom.
Perhaps the moribund would last a little longer
yet. Perhaps the cancer would lose the code.
Then what? The President goes nowhere
without the man carrying the football.
But that is no guarantee that
anyone will survive a first strike.
The paintings piled up. Someone would
have to investigate new storage.
But where? Who could build a rack
strong enough to bear such events
as the canvases imagined, then hid
to keep out the uninitiated, those
critics and pundits whom everyone sees
at openings, who put the drunken artists off
with their pickled scowls and solemnity?
But it was the way to go, filling the racks
until they groaned instead of the psyche.
Though unseen, it was destined to be
the best show in many a season. The work
would go on, as it always did, from there.
The President turned to wave as he
boarded a plane and everyone was dazzled.
Only a photograph recorded the other man,
unsmiling, standing with his briefcase.

DALMAN FLOWERS

I wrote the same poem twenty times
and tossed it out each time, unable
to figure out what I wanted to say.
It was in equal measure overwhelming
and vague, like a lot of things
having to do with origins, and both
the immensity and insignificance of people
for whom years proved a thicker blanket
than the ground ever was. I looked
at my model poets for guidance. Cavafy
suggested I use only small anecdotes
with sharp details—the rest would be
suggested through understatement.
Leopardi showed you have to notch it up
into the general air where individual
men and women lose their serial numbers
and join the human stream, at which
point your poem is a slow wail
of acquiescence. My poem began
with a man on an unpainted porch.
He was wearing overalls and looking
at the dry fields across the road. His son
would die of complications from polio.
His wife would succumb to a stroke

and die wedged between the refrigerator
and the kitchenette counter in a trailer.
He himself was awaiting earth departure
with Lou Gehrig's Disease. I remember
how he used the heel of one hand
to push the thumb of the other
in order to get the Pontiac door to open
in the hospital parking lot. I don't know
what put me in that scene, but to this day
the shock of that image still registers.
as does his floral name: Dalman Flowers.
And so I turn to Leopardi, where I find
sunflowers of the Marche buttering the fields,
as he set forth to find the troubles that fed
his real Muse, and the loss of identity
that gave him, in its place, a pure voice,
that made his sweet Silvia possible
and Romanticism itself—these things
waiting to meet him, later, in Rome.

David Rigsbee is the author of
The Pilot House, a Black River
Poetry Prize Chapbook (2009)
and *The Red Tower: New and
Selected Poems* (2010). Winner
of the Pound Prize, the Vachel
Lindsay Award, and a Pushcart
Prize, he has also been recipient of fellowships and awards from
the National Endowment for the Arts, the National Endowment
for the Humanities, The Fine Arts Work Center in Provincetown,
The Virginia Commission on the Arts, The Djerassi Foundation,
and the Academy of American Poets. He is 2010 winner of the
Sam Ragan Award for contribution to the arts in North Carolina.
Rigsbee is currently contributing editor for *The Cortland Review.*